Dedicated to my beautiful daughter Audrey and my husband Scott.

ααα

And much thanks to my friends who allowed me to use their faces.

Anthony Ortolano, Boo_kay, Patrick Roberts, and Alex Baker

Hope you enjoy ♡
Nasty

THIS FINAL HOUR

I hide in the corner

Under cobwebs

As demons swarm

The summer night

I watch them

As they sing off key

A sinister lullaby

Stealing fire

From candlelight

And like magic

Other universes

Appear in misty

Shadows dancing

On the lawn

A final party

In this final hour

Has finally begun

FALLING FACES

When I finally let you go

I let the whole world go

The light, the dark

The day, the night

Laughter and sorrow too

Cracks began to form

Threatening to swallow me

The fabric of my sanity

Was tearing at every seam

I fell into the starry sky

Grabbing at each point of light

When I notice other lives

Falling stars of fire grasping

A hysterical parade of faces

Looking for another life

CREATING FRANKENSTEIN

She gathered up her tools
Trying hard to make amends
Told herself she wasn't broken
That somehow she'd transcend
A few stitches to bind the seams
Maybe a patch or two to mend

Bleeding through her bandages
She's going through extremes
Trying to hide all her damage
Hoping to muffle all her screams

Too much time has been wasted
On trying to paint the perfect scene
The colors she used were bleeding
Into a predictable midnight screen
Too much time has been wasted
On memories she can never speak

Bleeding through her bandages
She's going through extremes
Trying to hide all her damage
Hoping to muffle all her screams

Every minute she is spending
On camouflaging her disposition
So much time spent on mending
Mirrors no longer reveal ambition
The scars she conceals are ugly
She is a Frankenstein to herself

ZOMBIE FOOLS

The moon watches

The sun looms

Broken bodies

March through town

Weaving through streets

Zombie fools

One by one

Side by side

Throaty moans

Escaping reality

Carrying nothing

But the torn shreds

They wore new once upon

The wind carried death

On slippery wings

The sneaky breeze

Fed the people

A sugary demise

They are aimless

Yet searching

I wonder where they'll go?

HER LAST GIFT

Tired she licks the salt from her lips
Blinded by a parade of ticker tape tears
Dripping in shades of black and crimson
Onto a tie dyed shirt she wore for years

She works her brush to busy herself
Applying pigments to imitate her emotion
She ignores the colored rivers on her face
Swirling strokes of sadness into her creation

Her tortured soul acts out in defiance
This last piece of art, this last conversation
Cancer making it too hard to do what she loves
Her voice given to those left with no direction

Whispering hope into colors thick on the canvas
Despite the pain washing through her brain
She thinks of her family, of all the beautiful love
And it's this love comforting her through this pain

She stands as she finishes, the last touch her name
Written with paint she mixes with her very last tear
She waits patiently until dry, then fits in in frame
Her last gift to those of life as death dances near

DARK SHADES

You lurk in dark shades of meaning

Realms of reality never your home

Comfort found in confused minds

You devour them feeding on hope

You gain strength inside angry desire

Welcoming them into white fitted arms

Feeling joy when they are weak

Too weak to beg for mercy

You are the demon born inside

The darkness of insanity

THE DARK NIGHT OF DEATH

The dark night held her in his arms

Weaving regret into her thoughts

Bringing to the surface old wounds

He covered her eyes with his hands

Blinding her to the light of the stars

Creating bleak and gloomy shadows

Macabre visions forming plans

Inspiring concepts best left buried

Raising notions from the dead

Of revenge and stained retribution

He sat looking at her, desiring her

Waiting for his darkness to consume her

Her tangible despair evident in her posture

Her eyes void of liquid strength

Fallen fall leaves stuck to her nude form

She looked for the moon but saw only death

Standing there beckoning her, consoling her

With one last search for a sign in the sky

She raised the knife and whispered goodbye

WORST KIND OF HUNGER

Her mouth a tempting blood stained red
Began to lure me spellbound into her bed
Her eyes like candlelight call me forward
Into sheets so black they looked like night
Her body a soft and stellar galaxy white

Her red lipstick drove me mad
Pouting at me all hurt and sad
I leaned down to kiss her ruby frown
And her full lips tasted like iron rust
A mix of torture and passionate lust

I remember my body felt rigid as anticipation grew
Energy felt alive and unfamiliar, something new
It began crawling beneath my skin, static electricity
It took over every organ rendering me carelessly prone
To an intensity that overwhelmed me, pulling me home

I awoke from the deepest and most traumatic of slumbers
Feeling lost and confused with the worst kind of hunger
Memories left to steal every ounce of desire I will ever know
The angel who had been buried in my sheets had flown away
Leaving me entranced by a silence that had nothing to say

YOUR FRANKENSTEIN

I change so often I can't see my image in the mirror anymore

In the beginning I was broken and you wanted to fix me

I was your project to heal…mend…bend to your molding

Faithful in every character, every need met with a smile

Your will was my command, I was a picture of your desire

Over time you would erase me, paint me in another world

Ask me to live as a different girl, you need something else

So time goes on and I become and become and become

Until becoming becomes angry and hurt and tired

And I become the Frankenstein of your creation

I become the girl without a face, the girl without a heart

ZOMBIE WITHOUT

I only met you yesterday
And today I don't feel too well
I think I must have left part of me
Because I no longer feel myself
I 'm now a Zombie without your love.

Not going to make it through this day
Left with no direction at all
Torn from life as I knew before
Consumed with hunger for your love
I 'm now a Zombie without your love.

I have a need and it's circulating in my veins
I have a need and it's overtaking all my thoughts
I have a need and it's consuming all of me
I 'm now a Zombie without your love.

Groans of heartache keep escaping my lips
Giving life to the death your absence left
Needlessly wandering, carelessly stepping
Vacancy filling my heart that is now bereft
I 'm now a Zombie without your love.

Don't tell me I'm one of a kind and that I am gonna be fine
Don't tell me there is a whole world for me to find
        because I'm not fine
Don't tell me I'm one of a kind and that i am gonna be fine
Don't tell me there is a whole world for me to find
        because I'm not fine

SEXUAL UNKNOWN

I got your hips locked hypnotic in a trance
My eyes pull you deeper with a gyrating stance
Feel my heart beat beat beating to our dance
You became my victim when I made my entrance

You're mine, you're mine mine
I'm a bloodsucker and I am making you mine.

My veins run toxic but pay no nevermind
I'm intriguing, appealing and seemingly refined
Ignore my enchantment meant to make you blind
Trust me I'll be gentle and ever so kind
So lend yourself to me and I'll help you unwind

You're mine, you're mine mine
I'm a bloodsucker and I am making you mine.

I'll steal your desire and make it my own
Instinctively craving my sexual unknown
The tension in the air begins to make you moan
I'll find a dark corner where we can be alone, alone, alone

You're mine, you're mine mine
From the very first dance
You're mine you're mine mine
I put you in a trance
You're mine you're mine mine
Take your body by storm
Invade your heart to death be reborn
Eat you up, beg for mercy, begin to pray
Forever after you will prey

You're mine, you're mine mine

THE PRESENCE I CAN SEE

I dreamed I was a little girl sitting in the dark

Of how I was supposed to be asleep in this dark

I dreamed of a faraway argument,

syrupy voices of familiarity

I dreamed I was not alone in this room filled with dark

Of how I sat with a presence only I could see in this dark

I dreamed this presence smiled at me,

comforting smiles of familiarity

I dreamed about the light this presence made in the dark

Of how it helped me feel safe enough to close my eyes in this dark

I dreamed of its love as I feel asleep,

heat filled warmth of familiarity

SHE IS A SKELETON

The future is owned and bound

Reliant on her

She sits in the closet

Recruiting an army

Thriving in the dark

Feeding herself with secrets

Slowly feeding the beast within

Guilt would die without her

She has a responsibility, a duty

To keep this beast alive

Because without shame

She would have no purpose

Her existence remains

As long as she can keep hidden

Collecting her secrets

When I am hurting…I reach out. I reach out in a very big, dramatic, vocal way. I write…I talk…I communicate. But when I am hurting I don't hear the responses, I see lips move without words, I get hugs that don't connect, I get love…that feels empty. I don't know why, I am in therapy for that. I do have haters…and there is a sick side of me that cares more for them than for my loving friends. I feel like they see me…their view matches mine. We seek to find evidence in the world confirming the things we believe. It is time I change the type of treasure I have been looking for.

THE DEVIL IS ME

There is a point…A very unstable point
When you realize "I can do this"
Or you decide "I won't do this"
There is a point when everything fails
Words stop having meaning
Comfort becomes mythical
For some reason the world
Becomes lonelier despite the people
The universe begins to swallow all meaning
And collapse feels imminent
That impending doom is inside of you
It gorges itself on your feelings
It hungers for dramatic emotion
This devil inside you binds you
As it distracts you from truth
It steals all logical focus and intention
Now down on my knees I wrestle
Spewing blame, anger, hurt
Trying to infect those I love so much
Gifting them apathy for part of my agony
This light of mine will not drown
The very end of me won't let it
It cannot be extinguished by water
It may look like a small burning ember
But as I shut down like a computer about to reboot
I will come alive with breath and a spirit
That will blow this small ember into a glorious blaze
I will not be defeated by the devil that is me

BOUND BY EMOTIONAL CHAINS

Imprisoned, incapacitated

Encapsulated inside a fear

Great and triumphant

In its overbearing ability

To consume the small

Left over hope forming

A shadow of existence

Lurking hungrily in

The audacity of

My meager intelligence

Trapped by its guile

And agile fragmented

Wisp of reality

I am branded

Like a hostage

Chained to the monster

Taking up residence

And living in me

DREAM ASYLUM

I had a dream
Filled with corridors
People without faces
Hunting for me
Roaming the hallways
Some of them sang
Poignant melodies
Echoing like heartbeats
Off the concrete walls
As I stood in the midst
Of my dream asylum
I saw a pair of eyes
The darkest shade of brown
Full of love or hate
No face there to tell me
The emotion they felt
Just eyes boring into me
Questioning me
Pleading with me
Hunting for me
Then as I stood confused
They blinked and disappeared
Leaving me with nothing
But the faceless creatures
That lingered looking for me

HIDING IN THE SHADOWS

I have discovered myself
Lurking in the shadows
Like a mass murderer
With a conscious
Trying to contain myself
The selfish tendencies
To lash out, to wound, to maim
With a hatefully sharp tongue
Prowling for victims
Curtains drawn, covers pulled
Hiding from the light of day
Worried for the whole of society
Embryonic hysteria hidden in fog
An absurd masquerade ball
Disguising the disorder in my mind
A part of me yearns to be saved
So I cry out from the shadows
Only to run and hide for fear
That Jekyll is really Hyde
Because in a moment of clarity
I know what is painstakingly clear
I must remain hidden to save you
From this possession that consumes me

MASK OF SANITY

Marketing sanity

Stable reliability

Clear eyes

With a hint of smile

Grinning checks

With a tad of blush

Lips made up

In glossy red

Clowns dressed up

Parading around

Jesters all of us

Performing

On a stage

Where our faces

Deny our insanity

MY PERSONAL ASSASSIN

It sleeps in my pillow

Waiting to smother me

Lurks in the shadows

Patient to swallow me

Lies inside puddles

Anxious to drown me

Lingers in the trees

Plotting to fall on me

Hides in my food

Hoping to poison me

Parked in my mind

Whispering to persuade me

Depression

The assassin inside of me

NIGHTMARE WITHOUT YOU

You're so far away
A place I can't reach
Desire aching fresh
Caught in its embrace

I can't feel your heat
Or the rhythm of your life
My bed remains empty
Something I can't seem to face

I try to imagine yesterday
The times I took for granted
The nights we slept ignorant
Of the empty space between

My pillow full of tears
Heartache my only lover
Grasping for existence
With you that can't be seen

Silence like an angry stare
Fills this dark room with regret
It screams of your absence
An unbearably quiet scene

When I can bare no more
I let out a anguished scream
And my husbands voice
Brings me out of the dream

DEVOTED APPARITION

You might surmise

Questions in my eyes

But all the answers

Led to my demise

My heart no longer beats

And long ago grew cold

It only half-lives

In your blood that flows

Now just an apparition

Waiting for you

Eternal in my love

Haunting you with

A surviving devotion

THE GHOST AND THE MORTAL MAN

Passion coursed hot

In loves everlasting chains

But now I stand watching

Through deaths revolving door

Glimpsing your emotions

You struggle to understand

Why I went missing

Stolen from our life

By disturbing circumstance

Of torturous cruelty

Now here we are never satisfied, hungering

A ghost and a mortal man, obsessed

Both separately reliving our last kiss

THE PREDATOR

When I shut my eyes

Your face terrorizes me

I don't know your name

But I know my demise

Your teeth are mangled

In the most sinister smile

Your eyes bloodshot

Fueled by a greedy insanity

Your callused hands

Etched by desperate pleas

Your laughter guileful

Echoing hatred

Feeding nightmares

Like the zookeeper of death

You are a predator

Hunting me down

To steal my dreams

HUNGRY EYES

I stood exposed
In the moonlight
On this foggy night
A midnight stroll
Led me to you
Crouching, watching
For me to notice you
I heard you breathing
My heart sped up a beat
And when I turned
I froze just staring at you
Your eyes hungry
Totally captured
Focused on me
My eyes stuck in yours
Trying to anticipate
Your next move
You had me in a trance
As you licked your lips
As if the taste of me
A mere second away
Something had frightened you
You were not yourself
Both afraid to move
You slowly stepped closer
Then bowed your head
And began to follow me

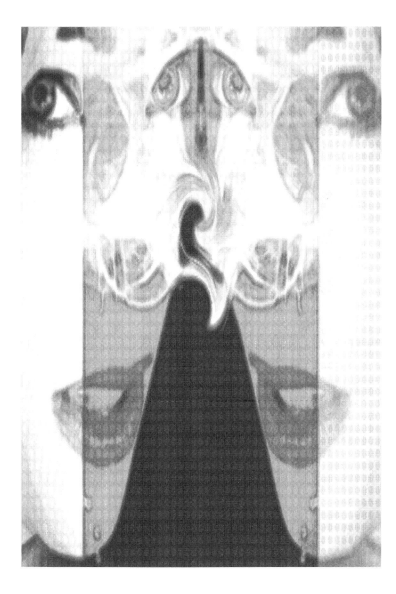

ICY FOG

An icy fog rolls in

Silently, beautifully

I watch it come

Over the land

In a meadow I stand

I watch it come

Mesmerized by its changing shape

Hiding its surrounding landscape

I watch it come

Anticipating the blanket of mist

And the secrets hidden in its midst

I watch it come

Longing for its mind numbing coldness

Sorrows devoured in abandoned boldness

                    I watch it come

THE DEVIL'S DOORS

I am standing in a row boat
In the middle of a lake
When the devil rises up
Lots of waves he did make
There are people on the shore
Watching as I struggle
Cheering on the spectacle
Placing bets among them selves
I can't tell who, too much fog
I can't understand them
Echoes confusing all they say
I hope she drowns I hear one say
Threatening my strength
As the devil looks me in the eye
And says," Yes you heard right"
With the smirkiest of smirks
I heard him in my head
Just stop and give up
You know I will win
Then before I could think
Three doors appeared
All made out of fog
Each one exactly the same
But for one single word

The devil laughed
It was his favorite game
"Well this should be good!"
He loudly proclaimed
Door number one said "DISEASE"
Door number two said "ACCIDENT"
Door number three said "HOMICIDE"
You get to pick your death
Know the way you will die
And his evil grin dripped
Hungry streams of venomous lies
Pick just one and I will set you free
Pick none and I will rock your boat
And drown the spirit residing in thee
"It will be suicide you see!"
I thought about this
And I thought some more
I could sense the impatience beginning to grow
I sat down in my little row boat
I picked up the oars
Without looking up
And without picking a door
I began to row
Because this is my dream
And I deserve better choices
I will be damned if I let anyone
                          limit my doors

THE MOON HOWLS

I hate getting trapped in my head
Worried about things not said
Pain of heartache, risk of injury
All things I historically fled
It's true I give more than I take
Even with everything at stake
But sometimes I am surprised
And the reciprocity is not fake
The silence, the quiet, the things unsaid
Begin to tell a story too often told in my head
I have to run, get away from the demon
Tying me down and holding me in bed
The depression is contagious, a sickness
A painful existence that howls in the distance
There is no use in hiding, no place is safe
Chipping away any attempt at resistance
I feel too much it's been said and it's true
My mood sparkly and next black and blue
Numb is the only way I can handle such pain
It isn't fair to me and certainly isn't to you
Please understand when I shut down inside
It isn't you but the howling moon I hide
It batters me bloody with self defeating lies
My monster is real and hungry with pride
Chain me up, and leave me be
As I attempt to tame this horror in me

BEHIND MY EYES

Locked alone

Abandoned

Imprisoned

In this room

My thoughts

Free

To torture me

No inspiration

No motivation

Silence

So loud

It deafens me

No friends

No enemies

No existence

Apart from me

Trapped

Behind my eyes

I find my biggest fear

IS *ME*

HUNGRY SIN

It's irresistible
The deep dark
Muddy desire
Lurking around
In shallow pools
Of hungry sin

It crawls undetectable
Under tables and beds
Slithers with languid tendrils
Catching us off-balance
Wrapping us tight
With unexplainable need

Relentlessly pursuing
As its hunted game
Unrestricted, passions untamed
Enticing us with an energetic force
To color each tomorrow
With the most picturesque regret

GHOSTLY WHISPERS

Sometimes I can't see the good
Only the bad, in everything
There are voices calling my name
But all I hear is muted silence
I feel ignored in the choir of voices
Praise falls on a cold heart
A heart that beats slow and quiet
Enthusiasm for life stalled
I look desperately for reason

I remember words said
Words that meant the world to me
And then I see them said
To everyone else but me
And I cry thinking I believed them
And they were just words
Words on a page
A page erased, crumpled, burned

Friendships promised
They would never leave
They would take the good
They would endure the bad
But they walked away
Not a second glance my way

As I suspected all along
What I tried so hard to deny
Was that my bad, is too bad
My kind of bad is like an anchor
Pulling everyone down around me
To drown in a violent cold sea

I hear ghostly whispers
I am important
I am beautiful
I mean something to someone
But it is hard for me
In the darkness I sit
To hear past the walls
Depression has built

BLACK WITHOUT YOU

Church bells were ringing gloriously
Somewhere beyond these pastures
The hills really rolled around here
In all directions to nowhere
We sat together in wheat fields
Listening to distant children play
While we hid from our parents
And slept in the open air all day
Topics of conversation flowed
Effortless towards the lazy sun
We shared secrets and fears
With the eavesdropping wind
We kissed once and felt silly
Content with holding hands
Today I lay in the meadow
Listening to the church bells
Sing a more melancholy tune
The skies are black without you
The boy I once daydreamed with
Was being prepared for eternal rest
Under the farmland we called home

A DANCE WITH SIN

Sins accent is thick and heavy
Its eyes are dangerously dark
It wears such a sexy smile
The kind I dream about
Sin begins to dance
Taunting me with its sex
Beautifully mesmerizing
Its body whispering in the shadows
Hands reaching for mine
And just like that
I am drawn into its arms
It holds me so tight
I can very barely breathe
For mere moments
Reason loses its focus
Logic's voice tries to surface
But noisy passionate lust
Veraciously preys on me
An insatiable sport
I desperately sink
Into a pitfall of desire
I cannot swim within
But happily I drown
Sucking up every ounce of sin

ICE MONSTER

It's as if you never saw me at all
An image inked in mundane hues
Part of a fabricated background
You painted over when you were through

It's as if you never saw me at all
A fable you made up and told a few
Fairy tales, lies, and some random news
I'm just another story for you

It's as if you never saw me at all
You left me a monster, pale and blue
Buried and frozen in a land of untruth
Left peering through a prison of lies

It's as if you never saw me at all
Labeled and branded cold as ice
Heartless I live beyond breath
My smile frozen in a time long past

DEAD PURPLE ORCHIDS

Dead purple orchids
Hang upside down
From passageways
Into right-a-ways
And veering left
Into alley ways
Roses without petals
Line the tile
The pavement
The travertine
Pricking feet
Drawing blood
Leaving trails
Of DNA
Of the blood of Christ
Of life
Paths and tunnels
Open and close
Widen and narrow
Keeping us searching
Keeping us hoping
Keeping us wondering
Where the sky has been
Where the stars hide
Where air blows free
Now that the sun
Collided with the moon
These dirt walls
Hold our destiny
Children of the dark
People of the night
The faithfully blind
Forever buried
Under a new world terrain
Prisoners held hostage
On a new enemy earth

DESTROYING HEAVEN

There was a hole in the sky
The universe was gone
No stars, no planets
No comets or black holes
It was just gone
I stood confused
Studying it
It looked very much
Like the eye of Jupiter
Swirling madly
A red churning storm
Angrily pulsating
Then an Angel appeared
And shook his head at me
"Sad you had to see this"
He told me a story
About how our emotions
Guide our actions
How they determine our fate
We used to live in a world of
Endless imagination
In a universe of splendor
Our love created beauty
In the sky, in the land
In the flowers and the sea

We are more connected
To nature than we believe
Love is magical
Hate…well
Hate creates disasters
It creates storms
Spreads diseases
Creates depression
Creates anger
Indifference, disrespect
A multitude of triggers
Set to detonate and destroy
The world we would love to see
With our own free will
We destroy heaven

VAMPIRE DREAMS

He saw writing on all the walls he passed
Heard heartbeats crying from her grave
Screams haunted every single dream
Walks the day knowing he was a slave

♥

To every hungry desire she ever had
Sacrificed his self to quench her thirst
And on his skin he bares the marks
Proving her love at its very worst

♥

Scars created in the darkest nights
Passion hotter than desert suns
Hurt so good leaving sheets shredded
A wild one with palm print buns

♥

A hunger that grew bigger than him
The beast in her unleashed a fury
She was an insanity he craved
Never had he felt such beautiful glory

♥

It was her punishment he desired
It was all he ever needed, destiny
But she went on the hunt for more
Her appetite grew too big, jealousy

♥

Caused him to step over the line
He destroyed her, a stake in the heart
And now he sits alone, listening
To her cry for the rest of eternity apart

THE DARK MAGICIAN

The dark magician came
Though I couldn't see him
I felt shadows gathering
Spells would be cast
Lives would be altered
Witnesses gathered
The spectacle would be grand
An island of eyes
Staring straight at me
My tongue was tied
Using a variety of lies
The magic of deceit
An illusion started
By a demonic fleet
Heavens opened up
And the rain beat down
Running mascara
Down terrified faces
They cowered under showers
That dampened their torches
Witches kneeling
Magicians begging
As I smiled and regained
The mind they had seized
So with these tears
I wash away
Whatever sorcery
Depression brings
Until the battle
For power
Begins yet again

THE DEVIL CAME TONIGHT

Deranged senses hunting

Peering through glass

Eyes transparent

Weaving lies into fear

Hiding behind a mask

Worse than a monster

The devil came tonight

MORTAL PAWNS

His enraged eyes settled on her

Spitting jealousy into creation

A loathsome disgust for humanity

Grown from an angel's insanity

Legions were born in his animosity

And deceit was served silver plated

Cloaks of doubt spun into veracity

Speared on hideously forked tongues

♦ ♦ ♦ ♦ ♦ ♦ ♦

Over time symbolism muddied waters

Spreading ripples creating the timeliest

Of providential distractions to the masses

Disguised within a religious masquerade

They misdirect the demented and deranged

If you watch you can see them pass by

An army of rebellious spirits in battle

Fastening strings on mortal pawns to master

UNTIL DEATH

From the very start

Until the very end

Battles are waged

Begun and finished

From the first breath

To the very last

It is a fight until death

SCARECROWS

We died bound
To wooden posts
Scarecrows
In a barren field
Long ago scorched
By desiccated air
And a blistering sun
Dry eager earth
Yearning for rainfall
Longing for spring
Aching for opportunity
A desire to live
To create life
The fruits of our spirit
Were picked apart
Devoured by visitors
Trampled by trespassers
Our salvation
Our destiny
Our legacy
all
Evaporated dreams
Because even together
Side by side
We were apart
Looking for answers
In opposite directions
In the end
Nothing good was left
The kind words silent
Sentiments had eroded
By wasted time
And we died bound
Next to each other
On wooden posts
Hungry for a love
We never found

FORKED TONGUES

Rationality stretches
into cotton candy strings
sweet and fragile
falling and melting on
snaky forked tongues

Cloudy tears well up
inside fragmented eyes
blurring perspective
and tainting perpetuity
into oblivious confusion

Sirens scream hysterically
as darkness descends
obscuring the dragon
as it feeds its hungry belly
on all of our inequities

ESCAPE

Tonight was the last night
T-shirt, shorts, socks
Bag of her dolls packed
The sounds of fright
Filtered each night
Into her dark room
Obscenities shouted
Phone calls disconnected
Dishes shattering
Late night callers
Sometimes policeman
Sometimes screaming
It wasn't fair
She was growing up here
Tonight was the last night
Tiptoe, listen, sneak
Through the back door screen
Into the dark of another room
One with stars and a moon
All she needed now
Was a kind loving soul
To take her in, to love her
No more padded rooms
No more treatments
Just a new family
New victims
For her to slay

MY FRANKENSTEIN

I want to tear you to pieces

And put you back together

Your hero, your love

Your ever-after

My forever Frankenstein

I AM EVE

Piercing judgment falls
Like burning embers
From a flaming heaven
The need for love
Imperfects us all
Driving us ambitiously
Into passions pitfall
Hold on to sanctity
Until it drives you mad
Strive for saintly
Until you lose your head
I have bonded with Eve
I have seen the fruit
Resistance is a lesson
Of ultimate futility
To be human
Has always been
Our intended destiny

WEDDING BURIAL

Spread your fiery wings over me

Keep pushing me into inky shadows

Towards the soft crumbling edge

Of the open grave you dug for me

The white dress I wear for you

Turns your frown into a smile

As you think of how the dirt

Will darken it, ruin it, destroy it

Destroying me was your fantasy

The dream you held for so long

This lacy dress draped in pearls

Is sadly

The purest thing about me

The only shred of innocence

Still clinging to me

Is this wedding dress

Worn for death

DARKER SIDE OF NIGHT

Selectively I grasp for substance, denying random meaning flaunting itself before me. Attracted to the darker side of night…waiting desperately for the moon to shine its light upon the faces looking up from their grave. Rising from death they grip you like a vise and bound you to eternity. Control within your reach waiting for you to realize death is a fairy tale. Expression of abandonment silently drowning in a sorrowful pool filled with crazy clouds of reckless blunder. Then as the moon begins to disappear the daylight begins to break through the dark exposing those things lusting in the inky black. It brings out the smiles that belong in the light and spreads warmth making the dark slink away back into the night.

THE MAGICIAN

I was doomed

The minute I saw you

Held hostage

Frozen inside

Icy shades of blue

I fell to my death

The day I met you

A prisoner

Restrained inside

A love that wasn't true

You played magician

I played dove

And once you held me

Darkness inside

Buried the sky above

No more skies

No more freedom

No hope of love

It was the price

You charged

To be a part

Of the show

Proof

Made in the USA
Charleston, SC
07 October 2013